This book is written by

_____

You are good at

_____

You always help
me to

_____

I love when
you cook

_____

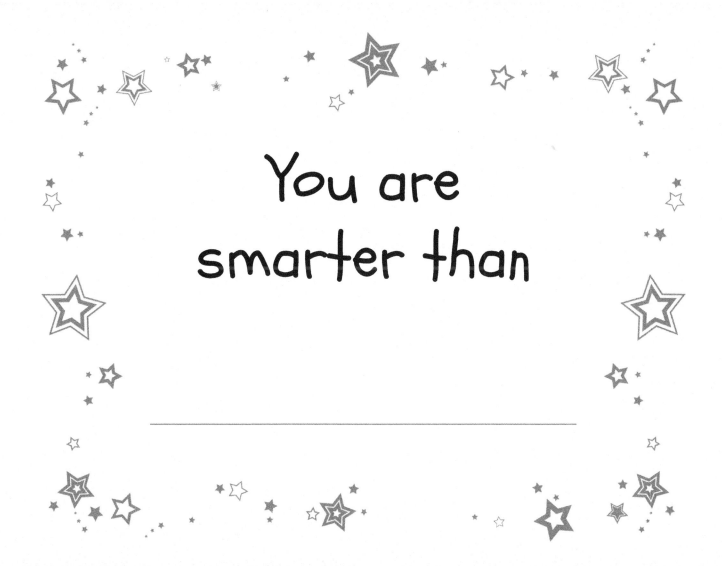

You are
smarter than

_____

My favorite thing
about you is

_____

If I had million bucks
I would buy you

_____

I like when you
call me

_____

Our favorite thing
to do together is

You are the happiest when

_____

Your favorite food is

_____

Tv show/movie that we both love is

_____

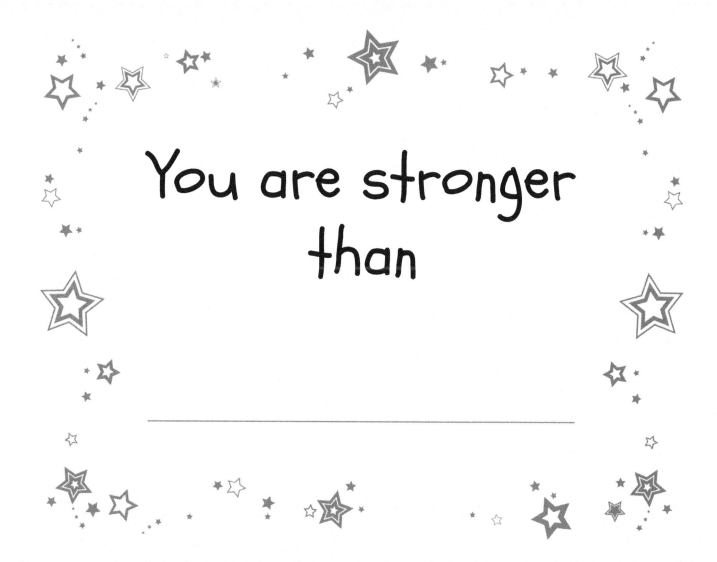

You are stronger than

_____

You are special to me because

You make everyone

_____

You taught me
how to

_____

I love when you tell
stories about

_____

You inspire me
to do

_____

I enjoyed a lot when
we went to

_____

I love when we prank

_____

I love you a lot
because you never

_____

Funniest thing you do is

_____

I wish we have more time to

_____

I feel safe when you

You don't care about

_____

I like when you
make funny

_____

I loved when you
surprised me with

_____

I love you
more than

_____

Game I like to play
with you is

_____

You are proud of me
when I

_____

I want you to
know that I will

_____